What to do and what not to do
to make life easier for yourself at work

What to do and what not to do to make life easier for yourself at work

Al Kelly

London · New York · St Louis · San Francisco · Düsseldorf · Johannesburg · Kuala Lumpur · Mexico · Montreal · New Delhi · Panama · Paris · São Paulo · Singapore · Sydney · Toronto

Published by
McGraw-Hill Book Company (UK) Limited
MAIDENHEAD · BERKSHIRE · ENGLAND

07 084429 1

Printed and bound in Great Britain
by Alden & Mowbray Ltd at the Alden Press, Oxford

To Ria

Contents

Introduction

We have all read about managing others—what about the beam in one's own eye?

This book will help a manager to succeed while making life easier for himself. It will not take the place of genius or outstanding talent, but it will put a man ahead of his intellectual peers. It will not make him match those who excel in one particular facet of the work but it will give him an above average score in all facets.

It will show you how to manage yourself, how to interact positively with those around you.

Acknowledgements

To all those interesting characters I have met.

To Jim Williams who suggested I should give a talk on this topic.

To Kay Harpur and Brid Tunney who put it in typescript and corrected most of the errors. Can you spot the deliberate one?

1. *Time Strategy*

Starting right

Tackle the hardest and most unpalatable jobs *first thing* in the morning; what a pleasure the rest of the day will be!

- interview that complainant
- do that difficult calculation
- read that long report or specification

The unpalatable task has a knack of getting covered up on the desk. Sure you intend doing it in five minutes time; but by choosing a simple problem first, you've lost the day's battle. The nasty is often the thing you don't excel in.

Repeat the rule after lunch.

After a while, operating in this way, nothing will daunt you; your confidence will grow and your output increase. If you pick off the cream first, all those cruel tasks will accumulate. You may be the only satisfied member of your department, but it won't last; the dogs will be yapping at your heels.

Don't think that by putting off tough jobs you won't have to do them; they'll be taken on by someone else, or blow up into a crisis. This is a fire brigade tactic; once you get to this state you'll spend your time putting out fires. You may think you're busy, but it'll be your own doing. What was that about a stitch in time . . . ?

Action guidelines

List on a small pad the tasks outstanding, and tick them off as you do them. Make a decision on every single item that reaches you, on the day you get it, without fail.

DO IT NOW. Not this afternoon or tomorrow. If you devote x minutes the first time you see it, and x minutes the second time, and if the time it takes to do the job is $4x$—you double this by putting it off four times.

Take an average day of 160 three-minute tasks. If you defer each three times, at one minute per deferment, you'll never get through the day's work and you'll get progressively more disorganized and useless. Consider how disastrous this can be: you take twice as long as you should on each item. In two days, you are one day behind. In six months, you are three months behind. In a year, you should be sacked.

If you're in a job where delays will never be noticed and where you have nothing much to do, what on earth are you reading this book for?

Don't try to keep the wolves at bay by sending memos or notes promising action on a certain task later. Back goes the task to the bottom of the pile, to become that much more difficult to tackle. 'No hurry—I wrote about that one a few days ago'. (Would you believe two months?)

Don't miss deadlines; otherwise, how can you in all honesty hound anyone else to meet their's?

If you get a query which has to be answered by this day fortnight don't put it aside. You'll have continually to remember to do it, and it will cross your mind several times in the interim. The date given is the *latest* date. Occasionally tasks will prove tougher than expected, so give yourself elbow room.

Get cracking one minute after you get to the office. The best half-hour's output of work is in this quiet time before the phones start to buzz. It's the best way to prevent an accumulation of work.

Never read a newspaper in the office—unless, you're the financial director and have to study *The Financial Times* or the *Wall Street Journal*. There are no ifs and buts about this. If 16 people read their newspapers for half an hour each morning, you can do without one of them and ban newspaper reading. Everyone knows they shouldn't do this—you can see how sheepish they look when you catch them in full scan.

'Never take work home . . . '

Don't take work home; it will become a disease. You'll stuff all sorts of unpleasant tasks into your briefcase and when you get home you'll find Johnny has the measles, and then friends drop in. You'll arrive back in the office with the briefcase unopened, and the merry-go-round begins again. This is escapism. Put nothing in a briefcase—DO IT NOW. Every day is not crisis day, so if you take work home regularly, you're not fit for the job. (In a new job, this rule can be broken for a short spell of a few months). Conversely —no personal letter writing in the office.

Be at work before, or at least as soon as, your staff every morning, even if you were a bad timekeeper in your youth. If you're not there first, you can't chastise anyone else for bad timekeeping or mitching. It weakens your whole position on malingering of any kind. Who says you may arrive late? You are smug about working late every evening, but this drives your staff mad to see you arrive late when they have been hard at it half an hour before you got in. And so do all those queries you ring them about right on quitting time! You're out of sync so get back in line.

Go home at quitting time. This will force you into getting through the day's tasks on time.

Telephoning

Always answer the phone on the first ring. You'll be thinking of two things while it's ringing and that's like trying to whistle and eat a meal at the same time.

Why fear you'll miss something by letting your secretary answer the phone when you have a visitor? Who do you hope it is? The managing director on to a wrong number who may be impressed by your brief mayfly moment on the phone? Never letting a caller on to anyone else is a 'grabbing' disease. Even with a visitor in your room you don't want to miss a chance to shine. This is discourteous; the caller gets preference over your visitor.

Switch the phone over to your secretary. If she's out of her room, answer the phone immediately with 'Can I ring you back, I've got someone here'; don't wait to hear half the caller's story. It may be a long one and the storyteller will only assume you wanted to find out which was the more important, your visitor or he. If you hear the story out, you insult your visitor. So either way you can't win; you'll waste the time of one of them.

If the phone rings just as you leave for an appointment, don't answer it. You'll be late for the appointment, even if you only tell the caller you have no time to talk to him. Throw the switch over to your secretary. How many meetings of a dozen people have to wait for one person delayed on the telephone?

When you get Bert on the phone, don't discuss the number of times you rang before you found him in.

- ❷ I left a message with your secretary to ring me
- ❷ I tried to get you when I got your message but you had gone to lunch

Make sure your secretary recognizes time-wasters who ring in from outside and protects you from them; if they insist, have her put them through to you 'at a meeting' or 'with someone'.

Don't make excuses; don't tell callers how busy you are:

- ❷ there is nobody here today but me and . . .
- ❷ all our records are all over the place
- ❷ this is one of a dozen similar calls I've had today

- they've decentralized my drawing office
- my secretary's out today and I have to answer three phones
- can I call you back tomorrow?
- we really have a staff crisis here today

All these were trotted out to me in the course of one day; consider the total of such conversations blocking the telephone exchanges.

When you phone someone for information and find he has no idea of the precise problem, don't try to educate him. Thank him for his help and get off the phone quickly, to phone someone who may know.

Don't go missing

Never get lost—ever. If you are

- going to be late in
- mitching
- in another office
- in Germany
- in the toilet

let it be known. Do you know that some callers to your company believe that everyone is perpetually in the lavatory?

In the case of a room housing several persons, it is useful to place a board by the exit and have each note the address or phone number of whoever he is visiting—or an x if he's in the men's room.

Do you think you can float around like a butterfly? If you do, people will treat you as such.

'Do you think you can float around like a butterfly . . . '

Silence is golden

Would you ever shut up!
Never talk at length at work about

- motor cars
- golf
- horses
- girls
- television programmes
- Northern Ireland, Vietnam, Berlin,
  or Pakistan

And note: bores who talk on and on about work are just like golfing or sailing bores: they don't even listen to other enthusiasts. It would be enlightening to tape-record four bores—a golfer, a bridge player, a sailor, and a fisherman, and then to record four bores on work topics. No one recognizes his own failings. Separately, each complains bitterly about other bores, while the rest of us snigger. But how do we know we're not in the same category?

It should rarely be necessary to spend more than five minutes talking to anyone about anything. Remember when you sat exams how much you could get through in five minutes? Step up the tempo.

Why gossip about the old days? Nobody is interested in what happened 10, 15 or 20 years back. It's the sure sign of a bore. It is not relevant and the analogies you use to try to put over new technologies are pathetic to younger technocrats. Better admit your scant knowledge until you can bone up on it (if ever). People approaching retirement seem to be convinced that development slows down as they close up to 65 and stops thereafter, so after 60 they specialize in 'engrossing' younger staff in stories of the good old days.

Face to face

See everyone that wants to see you NOW, not in half an hour or an hour. If you see him now, a sense of urgency is immediately communicated—he has to grab his stuff and hare along to your place. If you see him now you won't have that extra appointment cluttering up your memory load for the next half hour. A sense of urgency will speed up discussion and its termination.

Never sit down in anyone else's office when you can avoid it. Standing lends a sense of urgency. If invited to sit down, sit forward on the seat for a quick getaway.

Don't apologize for anything you are doing or proposing. Don't say 'sorry to bother you' or 'sorry to interrupt'. If it's true you shouldn't . . . if it's not true, go ahead without padding it out with apologies.

Start at the most recent part of any problem, and only go back as far as you must under questioning; this gives minimum time usage.

Don't keep opening up a problem. Maybe you intend impressing your audience with its complexity before giving it the *coup de grâce*. But they won't be impressed—just watch them fiddle with their pens, or doodle.

Some people complicate a problem in such a way that it can't be solved quickly, even if it's a simple question of the colour of office desks. This 'talent' can land you with 'If we get brown desks Jones will resign; if we get blue desks Smith will leave'. Don't mess around with it. Get Jones and Smith in fast. By calling the bluff such 'impossible' problems will cease to be put to you.

Short-circuiting long talkers

Visit Mr Talkative in *his* den; you can leave when you've got the information you want. How many times had you thought he was going out of your door when he came back in again?

Invite others at 11.10 if Mr Very Talkative is due at 11. Invite them in—'we are just finished'. If really desperate, invite another person along at 11.15.

Make a summary of the discussion and agreement or decision when Mr Talkative has taken up enough of your time:

❍ right then, we're agreed that you'll produce by Monday the sales forecast for the six months concerned.

or

❍ OK . . . here are my requirements of staff for the next

three years set out by category. Will you please set down recruitment needs for this period allowing the normal historical percentage for retirements of any sort.

If you've tried more than one summary and Mr Talkative is still in full spate, some more drastic action is needed: get taken short.

On the shop floor march smartly up to the person you are meeting, and if he is one who usually wastes time, intersperse such remarks as:

- ◑ I don't want to take up too much of your time
- ◑ I must not keep you from your work
- ◑ I must not delay you
- ◑ (looking at your watch and gasping) my goodness (or other suitable expletive) I'm late again (and dash off)
- ◑ I'll be along in a moment, Jack (catching the eye of a machine attendant).

Making every word pay

Jolly fellow Alf—he tells funny stories every time you visit him. Why tell them on the job? There is a place for them— off the job.

Never use the expressions (or allow yourself to think that) 'nobody ever tells me anything around here' or 'I've never heard that'. Darn it, the guy is trying to brief you and you won't let him. Let's face it, if you're worth telling—if it's not a hopeless waste of time trying to get you to help solve a problem—you'll be told.

Leave gaps in the conversation. It's no virtue to fill them unless you're helping substantially to reach a rapid decision. This rule is more dfficult for people reared in a talkative society—normally the south of each country and the cities. Country folk are used to long silences and are not terrified of them.

When anyone joins you and a colleague while you are in discussion do NOT NOT NOT say 'we were just discussing . . .' Now you have a third party talking about something, although he's not vitally interested in the end result.

As a corollary—if you are the third party, keep your mouth shut no matter how tempting it is to enter the fray. If you believe the result of the debate is crazy, tell the person left with you at the end of the discussion, and leave it to him.

You know people who spell out about three-quarters of a complicated story and then say they're going to write to you about it anyway. The poor fellows think they've got the toughest job in the world.

Waste no sympathy on those whose work is complicated by . . .

- ◑ someone should have a look at . . .
- ◑ am thinking of setting down . . .
- ◑ must get someone working on . . .
- ◑ it will depend on what comes up
- ◑ problem has got more complex since last meeting

Making appointments

Have your secretary make appointments for days when she knows you are in, but not busy—and without referring to you.

If *you* make appointments, always put them in your diary on your desk as you make them, so that your secretary will not be confused.

Cram lots of appointments into certain half-days, thus

making sure that the stream of visitors chase one another along.

Correspondence do's and don'ts

Insist that everyone sign and mail his own correspondence with the exception of:

- ➋ matters that are out of step with defined company policy (and you'd better define it in all important areas or you can't blame anyone for errors)
- ➋ letters critical of anyone outside your company or any part of your company outside your control
- ➋ anything that, in the judgement of the author, needs to be shown to his superior

The second will ensure that fiery individuals will keep their shot overnight before they send it to you for checking. Releases in the heat of the moment will be eliminated.

The last is very useful. It will identify the man who is afraid of his own shadow, and the man who never shows anything and so should be checked on once a year.

Never sign outgoing mail other than your own personal work. If you do, the author is annoyed, the recipient confused, and you are a fraud.

Have 'Joe Smith' typed below the signature on outgoing mail. Joe's scribbles are infamous.

Have all incoming post sorted and sent direct to the person who originated the correspondence. A simple reference system PR/JS/1247 ensures that the reply goes straight to Joe Smith in Production on job 1247.

Don't have all queries for their departments funnelled through you. That's a messenger's job.

Trust your secretary. If you want to open your post every morning—get a job in the mail room. Have you ever noticed how unimportant 50 per cent of the mail is?

Rules
'confidential'

❍ is the sort of item your secretary can deal with, and sign the reply for you. It invariably arrives from the personnel department

'The sort of item that arrives from your personnel department.'

'private and confidential'

◑ is just the same as 'confidential', but the sender is a bit younger and fancies himself as a secret service agent

If there is something that only your sacred eyes should see, it will be sent over by runner; this will happen once in two years.

Write short letters and memos—never more than one A4 page.

Don't write a letter in reply unless it is necessary to keep the original. Write a brief answer on the end of the incoming letter and post it back to the sender. It is no longer rude and is practised by many large organizations on their external correspondence.

Handling representatives

See only those representatives that you alone should see, and who offer something you really require.

Never see a representative because his company sent, or may send you, a Christmas gift or stand you a dinner.

Never see a representative because you did business with him in a previous, junior, post. The man who took your job will think he's being pressurized by 'old pals'.

Don't lunch with a calling representative unless you have been working with him all morning and will be working with him all afternoon. Chances are you'll be asleep from too much food and gin about 3 p.m. Even if you are to work with him later in the day, make some good excuse to skip lunch. (For the personality that repays with interesting conversation, do occasionally break this rule).

Command meetings: when, why, and how

Meet those reporting direct to you regularly—every four to six weeks, with a formal agenda. This produces team effort and makes sure that everyone appreciates the group's activities and problems. These are command meetings where *you* will have to rule on anything not agreed by all.

Are you afraid of meeting those reporting to you at regular sessions? Those who are usually argue that they see their subordinates regularly anyway, so why gather them together? Sure, you may lose face occasionally because two or three of them will get together and beat you over the head on something on which you haven't a clue; but look how essential that is.

At command meetings, tasks are handed out for the next period. Give yourself a fair share, and get all yours done in double quick time. Your tasks should be those that can't reasonably be done by anyone else.

Set a time limit—one hour is sufficient 95 per cent of the time—and stick to it. If any longer, the time will be taken by people not reporting results but trying to work problems out in public.

Insist on similar command meetings lower down the line at regular intervals, run by managers in each group— with agenda and minutes. Sit in occasionally when things are on target, to find out how it is being done. Sit in on *many* when things are critical or not going well. If the problem spot is far away geographically, don't miss a meeting for that reason. Your presence makes for extra effort to impress—it's as simple as that. The rivalry to 'produce the goods' at such meetings will help the job along enormously. It's amazing what gets done in the hour before a command meeting.

Insist on similar command meetings higher up the line which you should attend. If not held, nag till you get them.

Remember that the flow of commands and information up, down, and across occurs best when organized in this formal way.

Have a few small (2–3 persons) working parties reporting by a set date on specific problems, but remember that decision-making rests with the manager calling for the report, NOT WITH THE WORKING PARTY.

The art of the 'Quickie'

If you want a quick meeting, be there one minute before the due time: if you arrive 15 minutes earlier, you should be doing more useful work elsewhere.

Never be late.

Don't put off the fixed date and time even if you have to skip something that sounds interesting. The reason people do this is usually to justify their belief that they are more important and indispensable than those inconvenienced.

Set a starting time of 11.45; the intimation is that it must end at lunch-time—12 or 12.30.

Don't think you're required to lecture on every topic because you are sitting at the head of the table. Some chairmen are so ineffective that they blather away for 75 per cent of the time. It is astonishing the way perfectly meek committee members blossom forth into professional bores once they take a chair.

If you arrive late to chair a meeting it will lead to:

❂ someone else carrying on until you arrive

❂ your asking 'how far did you get' and then having the

meeting go back over the whole agenda to see what was decided

◑ your adding your own comments and the whole meeting having to start afresh

General meeting procedures

Have an agenda circulated beforehand: not one day, but three or four days beforehand.

Don't use an old-style agenda with general headings that could mean anything, like

◑ Production
◑ Distribution
◑ Sales

Rubbish!

Don't arrive laden down with files, books, pencils, papers. It shows confusion and lack of a positive system. Homework should be done before you leave your office.

If members don't have all the data they need, don't hang around. Set a time and venue for another meeting and get out; otherwise you'll finish up working out their data for them.

In a working party, don't let the most senior person take the chair. He will then act only as chairman to sum up the discussion and enumerate the decisions reached. The meeting won't turn out to be a command meeting.

Say the minimum and NEVER NEVER NEVER hog the conversation. Listen to the point of view of others and when you *do* talk, you'll command attention and respect. To see the truth of this, consider those whose opinion you respect, and think how little they talk at meetings.

Shorten the meeting by agreeing with anyone tending to reach a sensible quick solution, rather than taking issue with those going off at tangents; leave them there to return if they please. Fight the temptation to follow Alice into Wonderland, or you'll get lost too.

Decisions can be reached on a basis of 99 to 1, or 51 to 49. If you see it as 49 to 51, there is little point spending time pushing the difference of two. But if it stands at 25 to 75, the difference is too great to be a matter of opinion. Some facts are missing, so get someone to supply them.

If you talk too much at meetings the others will be thinking up clever contributions they'll make as soon as you dry up. They'll only half listen to your meanderings. The meeting becomes a chess game, with each protagonist more interested in his second next move than the current moves.

If the meeting is held in your office, at the conclusion get to your desk and on to the phone. The stragglers won't hang on for a chat.

One exception: meetings with trade union officials often continue through the lunch hour, so don't start them too early. Union officials need to report back on protracted negotiations through meal breaks, so respect these arrangements.

Fast, accurate, and useful minutes

Write the minutes—or have them written—*at* the meeting. Hand them to a typist on the way back to your office. If necessary, prolong the meeting by three minutes to do this. You'll save the time you would spend writing beautiful prose a week or month later. Better settle for poor style today.

(I admired individuals who were doing this for years, convinced that such talent was rare. Eventually, when I moved into a new post, I tried it, and the relief was enormous. Instead of arriving back at the office laden down with 10 pages of notes, I had handed over eight pages of minutes).

If you don't get minutes written at the meeting, you certainly won't want to do it when you arrive back at your desk and find all those messages waiting for you. Also, recording something you've talked at length about is dull and will be delayed for the slightest excuse.

Get the minutes circulated quickly. Minutes that come out a day before the next meeting are useless, and everyone else will be making their own notes to remind themselves what they must do. When they know they can trust your record, the meeting speeds up because the scribbling stops.

This writing of minutes has another virtue; it gives an excuse to stop the conversation wandering. You can butt in with: 'Well, ladies and gentlemen, is it OK to minute this discussion like this. . . .' This should stop splinter groups going off on side issue discussions.

Identify in the margin of all Command Meeting minutes:

   X For action by you before the next meeting
  XX For action by the divisional head before the next meeting
XXX For action by the departmental manager before the next meeting

It's amazing what will be done in the three hours immediately preceding the next meeting! And remember that nothing scores like good example. If you go back to the next meeting with any task undone you cannot effectively call anyone else to task.

Don't make notes of tittle tattle. The participants will wonder if it is to be used as evidence in court at a later stage.

Minute that 'B. Ragg stated he will have his work on Project A out by 14 July'. This pins him to a date. Set dates for everything and minute them for all to see.

If you are not recording the minutes, immediately anything is decided requiring action by you, don't make a note reminding yourself to write to A asking for the facts. Write the letter to A on the spot. This will help to

> ● keep the letter short because you have to pay attention to the meeting
> ● get quick action because you can give your draft to the typist on the way back to your office. She should be able to make English out of your bare bones.

Committees in-company and out

Have no in-company committees—command meetings yes— working parties yes—but NO committees. Otherwise no one person is responsible for the outcome and you will get the mess you deserve. If you want to stop anything happening, or to put off an evil day, a committee is useful. But a committee cannot control or build anything.

One committee, after a year's work, reported that, instead of doing what it was set up to do, it proposed to examine an entirely unrelated topic. There were some quite able persons involved, but a year is a long time and they simply avoided attending in the end, while the dregs of the committee gradually went off the rails.

I have seen committees that were effective; but when I checked up I found that one man did all the work, made all the decisions and printed results which the committee gladly endorsed as its findings; he could have had it finished in one tenth of the time but for the frustration of getting at least a decent number of meetings held; the drones love committees for the reflected glory; don't give them the chance. Give the task to the one man who can and will do the job.

The extreme case of inactivity is a 'committee' which meets to exchange views on the inadequacy of staff and budget to produce required results.

Don't sit on more than two amateur committees outside your job at any time; this includes golf clubs, social clubs, and professional institutions. If you do, you are a professional committee man who likes indecision and blather. Such committees off the job are harmless—the work is all done by one person in any case, but they will give you bad habits.

International conferences: when to stay away

Multi-lingual conferences are a menace; hundreds of delegates cooped up in theatres listening to simultaneous translations of lectures. The disease is that each delegate, through his earphones, has to listen to very odd translations into his language. I once jotted down the following in one 8-minute session:

- circumscribe the possible solutions favourably available
- characterized constraining factors within these structures
- depend on the wide influences of the restraining affecting factors
- on the basis of the conceptual acceptance of the regimes which are incidentally accidental
- the devices which are disarmed of the affections

Writing down this nonsense was the only value I gleaned from the session. So—be very selective about attending such conferences. Better to read the papers in good translations. Many conferences simply rehash previously published papers to keep a company name before the public.

Some world-wide organizations set up a momentum in conference holding—employing staff just to generate lecture sessions so that the income will pay for their services.

Be selective, very selective, with time-wasting conferences.

Cardinal rules of Chapter 1

DO	*DON'T*
◑ Most difficult task first	◑ See all incoming or outgoing post
◑ Stop talking	◑ Get lost
◑ Be on time	◑ Swop yarns
◑ Avoid Mr Talkative	◑ Have any committees
◑ Hold monthly short Command Meetings	◑ Postpone any meeting
◑ Write minutes *at* every meeting	◑ See representatives or have lunches that can be avoided
◑ Record specific tasks in minutes of meetings, with deadline dates	◑ Attend useless conferences
◑ Agree with others whenever you can to speed up meetings	

2. The Information War

Don't read anything twice—not a word or line or sentence. Train yourself to concentrate, not to think of golf or the family, or even the job, while reading a specific item. Avoid a 'Joycean' thought-process—thinking of forty different things while you skim through your correspondence and then find you've got to the end without getting the full import. Remember your school days.

READ THE QUESTION
READ THE QUESTION
READ THE QUESTION

Incoming mail

A pile arrives in the morning. How should you tackle it? If you have organized properly (as described elsewhere) what arrives *can* only be done by you and *should* only be done by you. So set quickly about doing it!

While every item must be dealt with today, it is allowable to go quickly through the pile first, pulling out items for really fast action . . . a simple 'yes' or 'no' scribbled by you for your secretary to handle. You will be left with the really important items. Get out the most difficult one first (see 'What to select') and then tackle the others.

Documentation and memos

All documentation should be read and dealt with in under

an hour—on most days half an hour should suffice. Otherwise you're simply reading what others are doing, and leaving yourself no time for your own job.

Don't handle any piece of paper twice. Never read what others should have received if it arrives by mistake on your desk. It may be darned interesting but resist the temptation and put it in the out-tray for the right person. If you read it you will think about it, talk about it, or—worse still—maybe even try to do something about it.

Don't read trade magazines just because they arrive on your desk. Remember that two dozen copies addressed to other managers have been received by the company. Let the man who must and should read them, do so.

The value of scintillating prose

Every writing job should be done once only . . . no revising, editing, or polishing. It's not worth it, and if you know there is to be no revising it'll make you concentrate better.

Don't make drafts of

- ๏ minutes
- ๏ agendas
- ๏ letters
- ๏ memos

This only doubles the work. What if it's not perfect? If it's sufficiently bad someone will howl. In practice, this will happen rarely: say 0·01 per cent, so why do 200 per cent to avoid that?

If you handle only one problem at a time, you'll become a blinkered horse. The laser beam mind, while impressive, is useless unless you are on a single research project with no deadline and no budget limit. People will forget you exist and the problem you're tackling will be forgotten, or done quickly by someone else. So keep all pots stirred.

If you have 20 current problems, give each a nudge often. The cook who can simmer soup, boil potatoes, roast beef, make gravy, steam vegetables, bake a pudding, whip the cream, and percolate the coffee—without burning, boiling over, or drying up anything . . . is the winner. If your wife can do it at home, you can do it in the office.

Sit down once a month and:

- ➋ check on what it was that took up so much of your time during the month. Can one general rule be made to avoid some specific tasks? If so, make the rule or go and seek agreement to it. Accumulate examples and battle ahead to get the rule accepted. One hard day's work now will save many over the next year. NEVER continue making repetitive decisions. Make one and record that in future you only want to see items that do not accord with that decision
- ➋ check on what regularly arrived in your morning post that was not your concern—magazines and literature that you re-addressed to someone else. Instruct your secretary to deflect all this in future
- ➋ write notes of praise to those who have recently deserved them

A note in your bring forward (BF) file is the reminder.

Check the minutes of the last meeting and have a standing instruction with your secretary to launch volleys on anything you are to attend to (everything marked **X**), and to mark in red on your copy of the minutes those she finds she cannot do. You can then personally wrap it up by closing time. In this way you do the least possible amount yourself. If the minutes read:

X Services division to be asked to move M. O. Ving on Tuesday 9 February

X A new management structure to be drawn up by 10 February

your secretary will do the first without reference to you, and mark the second in red for your attention.

To hoard or not to hoard

Keep your office tidy and uncluttered. No old calendars on the wall even if you like the picture. No college notebooks, magazines you piously hope you'll get around to reading one fine day, rough notes taken at meetings, anything belonging to your predecessor in the office.

If the calendar is out of date, throw it out—use your desk or pocket diary.

I've seen those who retired before they threw away notes of college lectures of 40 years earlier. You need to go deeper into any practical problem than in college days. (I had some notes for 20 years before dumping them reluctantly—unused—in the waste-paper basket, having coped with problems far more complex in the fields covered in the notes, by boning up on more modern methods and techniques).

Have a shallow—no deeper than 3 in.—drawer that locks, and don't put elsewhere any work that has to be done. You will be amazed how you will have to get rid of the rubbish. They say that if you keep something seven years you will find a use for it, but is it worth it if you have to wait seven years? You may not be there by then (you hope), and its technology will be obsolete anyway.

Don't keep anything in your desk other than papers collected for tomorrow's meeting or awaiting specifically requested data for work you personally (and no one else) is involved in.

Don't have a basket full of paperwork. This is the deep-litter system which produces good hen manure. Spend two minutes searching the litter for an item 15 times a day and your time is gone up in smoke. An extreme case is the man with a cupboard chock-a-block with papers, all awaiting decisions. I knew one so full you could not open the doors without causing an avalanche. Whenever I see someone putting papers into a drawer *during the day*, I get a sinking feeling they are being left there to 'ferment'.

'The deep-litter system.'

Don't have a basket, don't have an in-tray. Just let items arrive on the desk to be dealt with at once.

Do you hoard magazines and reports that you are going to read when you find time? You never will. Read them now, or send them to the library, or put them in the wastepaper basket. A good rule is to do this exercise the afternoon before holidays—at Christmas, Easter, summer—and dump 50 per cent of everything in the room. You've met the sort of man I mean—peering from behind a barricade of journals 'I'm going to read them when I get time'. The fact that he mentions them reveals his guilt complex.

If you haven't the courage to dump such valuable gems, then post off loads of them to someone else in the company: he'll do it without turning a hair.

Don't keep drawers full of papers that should be in the files. You're keeping them just in case you want them, but you never will. When you're away your boss and colleagues can't find anything, and this doesn't make you seem essential, just confused. Trust the filing system you've got until you get the chance to improve on it.

It's a mistake to keep a large cupboard in your office. It will fill up with useless stuff that will be thrown out on the day you retire (or die). Beat them to it and let the company benefit from the value of your waste paper.

If the cupboard has a glass front you may feel obliged to put in it rows of impressive looking tomes to look down on visitors. Anything more than one shelf 3-foot wide is unnecessary. Have a rule that any book, even if you bought it yourself, that you haven't used in the past six months should go to the company library.

Secretaries and other facilities

Dictate to a shorthand writer only at a time when you get no interruptions—the first half-hour of the day while lazier folk read newspapers.

Don't dictate unless it is absolutely necessary. If 'yes' or 'no' or 'next Tuesday' or 'set a date and time' is sufficient indication to your secretary, then for heaven's sake don't have her sitting there while you launch into:

Dear Mr Jones:
In reply to your letter of 16th inst., I confirm that we shall
issue you with our enquiry for . . .

You are wasting your time because 'yes'—in July' scribbled
on the arriving letter would suffice. You are wasting your
secretary's time because she has to take your prose down
in shorthand and subsequently type it. All your ahems and
pauses and phone answerings can stretch a simple letter
into ten minutes of both your times.

Use . . .

- a dictating machine
- a tape recorder. If you drive a lot on the job you will
  often think out solutions as you travel. To avoid having
  to recall these or stop the car to jot them down, record
  as you go
- intercommunication system in the office and/or factory
- push-button phone connections to those you deal with
  most often
- a switch-over phone which rings in your secretary's
  room and will be, by arrangement, answered by you
  only if it rings more than 3 times
- pocket locators for mobile staff—on a construction
  site for example. When you add up the cost of one
  journey a day to fetch a man all the way to the office
  phone, the cost of the equipment will be justified

Make sure that everyone reporting to you has secretarial
help, but not necessarily a secretary to every person—
except one with a fantastic output or who is so disorganized
that you must keep him in tow.

Have no copy typing; no checking is then necessary. Use a photocopier.

Have your secretary . . .

◑ Keep a record book on submissions and requests you have made, queries you have raised, letters you have sent which require an answer, so that you will NEVER have to remember to follow up on anything. Have your secretary do the follow-up, even if it is to the chairman of the company
◑ Chase up information you need—be it financial or technical—unless it is of great complexity
◑ Tot up simple accounts
◑ Give supporting information to help anyone to whom you have addressed a query. By building up confidence, these people will get into the habit of asking her for information, instead of asking you

You will seldom, if ever, get all the replies to a circular enquiry by the deadline you set. It's a bit like rounding up chickens at sundown; it's not always the same chicken that is last. Leave the chicken collection to your secretary.

Arrange offices so that people don't tend to chat. It's not a good thing to have four people in one office if they are engaged in work of a non-repetitive nature. One or two is better. A large number is OK provided you break up the area with potted plants and shrubs, and soundproof it, to turn it into a one-two arrangement.

Communication

Interview yearly everyone to 3 steps below yourself. You will then learn such things as:

◑ men underutilized; there under 'Parkinson's Law'

- incompatible personalities
- boss performance
- what you are not doing
- crying needs of junior staff
- uneven delegation of responsibilities

Have a news sheet run off which has anything that you or anyone else in the Company or Department thinks *everyone* should see; large orders placed or landed; competitors' or customers' failures or successes; coming change of office accommodation; interesting discoveries by members of staff.

Produce a house journal (preferably technical, to keep births, deaths and marriages from taking over) where *anyone* can write an article under his own name. Find out who has ideas or a knack for something and tell the editor of the journal to worm it out for printing. Be careful to get an editor who will keep the journal up to standard and on time, e.g. someone who collars you to ask 'Why can't we have a good technical magazine in this place?' Get the better stuff published in outside technical journals.

Make it the job of all who have information to pass it on—after all, who else knows they have it.

Hurlers on the ditch (I'm Irish), referees in the stands, will abound. They never take part in a game but can shout abuse at you any time you make an apparent wrong move. No one has the right to criticize after the act. If he has anything to say, let him say it in advance.

Don't try to issue the magazine monthly or quarterly. Come out in sequential numbers as the editor gets enough worthwhile information. Three per year for the first year and 1 or 2 thereafter should be enough.

Visit all plants, branch offices, subsidiary companies, at

least once yearly. It should never be possible for a complaint to be voiced that you have not set foot on the premises in two years. To get to the real problem—the one nobody will set to paper because it's dynamite—watch for the tip of the iceberg.

Don't wait for junior staff or managers to approach you—remember they may be scared to do so. OK, so you're the soul of kindness, but they don't see it that way, or believe it. Go and meet them. And don't say anyone is welcome to visit you any time and leave it at that. It's tantamount to saying 'I live by the Seine, you must drop in some time'.

Send copies of everything coming from the managing director to all your managers—unless the MD says not to.

Have a code your secretary understands for distributing MD instructions and information, e.g. 'TM' means 'Top Managers only'. It is better to over-trust your subordinates. If you ever have to apologize for sending them something they shouldn't know about, at least they'll know that they see all they should see.

And remember, the same information has probably reached the hall porter already, and your managers realize that you are hatching another egg.

Inform your subordinates clearly and regularly about the results of their own efforts. If you don't, they'll set up a spy system which will occupy much unnecessary time. Make it clear to them that if one of their projects has not been sent back within three days it is on its way to wherever it should go, board meeting or works management.

Have a House or Works Committee for discussions on anything of general interest to staff: facilities, future orders, staff requirements, staff training, but not on disputes.

Try to cut out speech mannerisms. How do you spot them?

By asking others, or by a tape recording. An extreme case is a person who repeats half of each preceding sentence, rather like someone trying to walk up a slippery slope. Other examples?

- on the other hand
- the point is
- you know
- I mean
- in actual fact
- sort of
- nicht wahr
- um . . . um

Mannerisms are not recognized by the user, but are distracting to his audience.

Don't be scared that someone else will make a sensible contribution to a discussion. I've known individuals who continually utter noises just to hold the floor.

Cardinal rules of Chapter 2

DO

- send all communications from the MD to all your subordinates
- have one very shallow locking drawer
- have one 3 foot shelf for books
- keep all pots stirring
- keep your office tidy
- let your Secretary do all reminders and answer all possible letters
- have an informal news-sheet
- have a formal technical journal
- have an office committee
- see personally each member of staff annually.

DON'T

- read anything twice— not a word
- have an 'In' tray
- have mannerisms of speech
- dictate simple letters
- keep anything for future reading

3. Secrets of Success

Tactics for change

When anyone says 'Why can't we do x' or 'Why does someone not do y'—immediately reply—'You do it and by what date can you do it' (unless of course undue resources are required). This sorts the men from the boys. The ones who complain 'nobody tells me anything' and 'nobody lets me do anything' are left behind by the genuine tryer who wants to improve things. It is the person who suggests the change who has the conviction to carry it through its frustrations to fruition.

Why resent suggestions for change? Sure it makes your job tougher but you are not here for the easy life.

Two companies that were supposed to have been 'merged', years later each had the same management structure, products—and losses. In a merger situation management goes on the defensive and if you don't act at once the defences will be impregnable a year later; you will have been proven too weak to touch them. You are expected to act immediately and not doing so gives hope that you are going to be weak; hope will strengthen opposition to change.

Don't think that development ceases when you reach your dotage. In fact it is compounding because it's a cumulative process.

Don't push, push, push until everyone is fed-up with you.

If you have a good idea that falls on stony ground wait for the Managing Director to ask for suggestions in a period of stringency and resurrect it in updated form. Remember that a creative person never stops with one or two good ideas; he can't win them all and if he scores with 8 out of 10 he should be pretty satisfied.

Don't hold a life-long crusade with which others don't agree. You'll just get nicknamed after your dog-eared idea. There is a limit of time and energy worth putting into any one effort to change; the effort to perfect an idea *privately* can go on intermittently for as long as is necessary. If no active support forms in 3 months from launching date opposition is strong and the change is probably not worth pursuing. To test the validity seek a patent (if it is patentable).

List *all* the cons as well as the pros; this scuttles the opposition as they can't add an iota against the plan.

If you have a novel idea and you are finding it difficult to gain support, use strategy: see if you can get an offer of publication as an article in a trade magazine; if you get the offer it confirms that your idea has some validity. Top management will probably have to read your article to give an *imprimatur*. How better can you get the Managing Director to read what you have in mind?

Have you this week changed a traditional way of doing something—by copying someone else, adopting a suggestion, or initiating a change of your own devising?

Consider a manager in 1920 who believed that he had the optimum solution to all his company's problems! Of course this can't happen now—we are in a more enlightened age?

Problem-solving

Put the problem being discussed right out in the middle of

the table for all to see and examine. It's only those who fear superior knowledge or observation who play problems like poker. This knack of coolly putting all the cards face up on the table is the hallmark of the winner. He has no time to waste playing the deuce of clubs and waiting to see what you will do. He leaves playing Snap to children.

Present the problem correctly in all details the first time. Remember that if you purposely leave one small area uncovered to avoid offending someone—intending to fix it later—that will be the *whole* problem next time around; it will grow with your blessing.

Get your facts straight, otherwise you will move with every breeze. The man who can be persuaded to do anything—provided that the opposition is kept from him—is no better than a tape recorder.

If there are 15 problems and 12 of them have been thrashed out previously, for goodness sake don't mention any of the 12 again. Some people revel in this. They think it makes their job seem more important; it simply makes them appear confused.

Why nail your shirt to a mast? You may see it in tatters before the day is out. Shirt nailers lose credibility, even when they have done their homework and are perfectly correct.

Don't plug or advocate any line of action that

➋ brings more work or power your way
➋ is glamorous in its sophistication

unless it positively is the correct thing to do. Show all the disadvantages and reasons 'why not' as well as 'why', otherwise your enthusiasm for progress and development will become a crusade, very often without followers.

Consider pros and cons *in toto* by writing them down to prevent your pre-empting the solution. All planning and decision-making should be done thus. It's not like backing a horse at a race track. It's more like a detective looking for the culprit—he must NEVER assume even on circumstantial evidence, who is guilty. This is a difficult discipline to master, some never learn it. No decision is based on 100 to 0 facts; an easy one is 70 : 30. Most are closer, otherwise you would not be calculating and discussing the matter at all—or should not be.

When you are ignorant on a problem, admit you don't know at once and ask if anyone present has the answer; 95 per cent of the time you'll find that the others will claim they were all just going to pose the same question. All my eye and Betty Martin.

Clear vision and straight action

Remember you can't win them all. An irate customer told one manager that the speed of his reply had proved the company was rotten from top to bottom!

Know the game you are in—go back to college or study to be on top of the job, otherwise you will be (not just appear to be) gradually more and more of a bluffer. I call this Presbyopia in Management. (Presbyopia = sight of an old man).

Don't make excuses:

- my report is not as exhaustive and complete as I would have liked. . . . (Quite the longest report I ever read was introduced like that)
- annual leave and pressure of work prevented us . . .

Never believe that decisions you have to make are tougher

than anyone else has to face; it's not the decisions that are more difficult—you are. Everyone's decisions, *if we are all in the right jobs*, are equally easy, from the office cleaner's to general manager's.

Never be deflected off the job in hand. If the task is to travel the shortest route between London and Glasgow don't stop off looking at cathedrals on the way; if you find yourself doing this it's a sure sign you don't like the rest of the journey.

Going off onto other tasks that are not appointed and not relevant is a common disease; it just shows you're afraid to tackle the job you have been given. You are simply, in your own estimation, clearing the ground to get at the job. You cannot be called to account for failure to excel in these diversions; you cannot be seen to fail in your main task because you have not begun it yet.

Avoid opening up problems any more than necessary by adding:

❷ what of the influence of z?
❷ should we consider y and z?
❷ possibly p, q, and r should be investigated?

This mentality is hell bent on turning one problem into 20. It is studded with 'might', 'maybe', 'possibly'—never facts and figures prepared in advance to help towards a decision.

Don't look for difficulties:

❷ what would b think if I did this
❷ I'd better chat this over with c

You just want an excuse to avoid making a decision.

Don't believe a salesman's unscientific forecasts of future business; he is a professional optimist.

Go for cold-blooded market-research, statistical-analysis forecasts.

Initiative

Initiate something every day. What else are you there for?

If you don't initiate and instigate, you are a constriction in the flow of work and decisions. By initiate, I mean start something which will result in improvement and work it out to a useful stage. I do *not* mean you should sit there firing off salvos

- why don't they do *xyz*
- what about trying *abc*

No management job should contain less than 25 per cent initiation and instigation, and the more senior the post the higher should be the percentage.

Containing your job

Confine yourself to those tasks that cannot progress while you are on holiday or sick. If it goes on fine when you are golfing why come back to re-do, comment, undo or, as others see it, mess up or slow up? This includes signing documents and forms that need to be approved by a person of your status; they'll get signed when you're missing.

Bring your expert along to any meeting on his specific area. If you don't you'll be seen as trying to persuade your boss that you are expert in this discipline, and your subordinates will be sure you'll mess it up.

Always refer your boss to one of your subordinates who knows the answer to a problem; NEVER, NEVER, NEVER act as postboy or telephone enquirer to get him the answer.

'Never become a PR officer showing visitors around.'

Don't become a glorified public relations officer

- attending official openings of new office blocks
- bear-leading visitors
- inspecting the plant as an interested amateur
- receiving representatives flogging equipment of marginal interest to staff three steps lower in the organization
- going to luncheons in the local Ritz every day and cocktail parties every evening
- attending funerals

Don't let yourself believe you have a whole-time job 'supervising' a dozen persons' work. They should be well able to get on without supervision—you thought you were before you got the last promotion.

Never do anything that could be done equally as well, or nearly so, or better by a subordinate.

Ask others what improvements could be made. Get, say, 25 suggestions, put in rough order of value, and tackle them. Get at least 20 done in a year. Review them each quarter to see whether any should be dropped owing to changing circumstances. If you get stuck at No. 2 let it simmer and carry on down the list.

Never deal in working hours with matters connected with outside activities:

❷ Professional Institution work
❷ Golf Club committee work

You may argue that this is useful to your company, increasing your influence and sources of information, but there are extreme cases of managers who do little else. The disease is rampant as managers become more senior, junior managers coming to believe that their seniors do little else but phone each other on committee matters.

Judgements and decisions

'Making decisions' simply means 'choosing a course of action'. Ask the janitor to decide whether you should or should not buy a new computer. He can say 'Yes' or 'No' and thus 'decide'. This is known as a guess.

What *you* should do is PASS WISE JUDGEMENTS and to do this you must hear the evidence of protagonists. In the case of the computer you must have set down all the problems associated with a YES and all the problems associated with a NO judgement. If you get a submission from the computer division recommending the purchase of new equipment with a long list of fantastic advantages—smell a rat; no single product has all those advantages or it would be the only one in use. What of the extra cost? The more expensive software? The absence of canned programmes on the design end of your business?

Any fool can make a decision. But who can pass a judgement of Solomon?

Making a decision does not finish the matter. Your subordinates will be back with further efforts to force you to a wise judgement. Do not think because you penned your signature to 25 decisions this week that you are proving your worth. Agreeing to (a) accept the cheapest evaluated tender, (b) appoint the man selected by the interview board, (c) pay the rate accepted in the industry, don't count as decisions. Are you left with any?

Remember, many decisions that company rules stipulate must have your signature *can* be signed by someone else in your absence. I've known submissions held back for months until a certain manager was on holidays—he was a professional 'No' man.

Of what is submitted to you, if you decide NO to:

20 per cent,	you have either a selection of idiots reporting to you—or you are one and don't know what goes on;
5 per cent,	you are asserting the veto to prove your presence;
1 per cent,	this is tolerable in a rapidly changing environment and the NO calls for additions or alterations before approval;
0·1 per cent,	this is about normal. The NO should normally be on something left open pending a YES or NO decision;
0·0 per cent,	you are a rubber stamp.

You should have set down rules to cover what normally reaches you in such a way that both you and the submitter know in advance what the decision is to be! Set rules for what is to be inspected abroad, for example, or how often contract meetings are to be held in the USA on a main contract; rules for assessment of tenders.

What to avoid in decision-making

Delaying a decision won't make it easier. Two conflicting views are with you for a decision—get on with it. If you wait until the last day you will be pressurized and appear to have panicked. Such delaying is often done in the hope that protagonists will finally agree without bothering you. Nonsense! Often they know what should be done but it will remove a degree of power from one of them; sometimes they have agreed privately what the outcome should be. You're in trouble if you rule the opposite way.

Delaying decisions is not going to save the firm money. If you hold up a £120000 decision for a month do you save the interest on the value (about £1000)?—No. The manager involved will have you sized up and will build a month's allowance into the time schedule. You are wasting everyone's time. If your subordinates have a BF file for your activities it is a very serious reflection on your efficiency.

Don't invent 'principles' to suit some *ad hoc* decision. A manager with a 'principle' never/always to take a certain line means that there is no reason whatever that can be justified, but he still likes the cut of it.

Don't be disgruntled if all the facts are presented to you on a plate and you have no comment to add. Agree on the spot. Don't feel superfluous.

Never make an arbitrary decision 'to put the other fellow in his place'. This is Army tactics and it's not an army you are in. Anyone of worth will never be put in his place!

Studiously avoid discussing matters in one of your subordinate manager's area with other subordinate managers. This is diffusing the problem and procrastination. The word will get back that you are trying to set one against the other and if they are men of honour they will not express amateur opinions on colleagues' work. You are trying to make peace between tinkers and they will both turn on you.

It is no excuse for delaying decisions that you:

○ had a strike on your hands; doing your ordinary work will keep you from worrying in between times about action on the strike;
○ were in Germany all the week; were you sleeping at the airports and on the planes?
○ all your assistants were down with the 'flu'; everyone is capable of twice the output normally achieved, so get on your bicycle.

Don't get scared and suggest

○ appointing a consultant
○ setting up a committee (see Chapter 1)
○ leaving it until the next meeting
○ thinking about it for a few weeks

Record-keeping

Have records produced (graphically) of the most important aspects of your work, e.g.

○ Programme
○ Cash Flow

and keep the staff hot with queries if off-schedule twice in succession as reported at selected (say monthly) intervals.

Home-in on faraway budgets. 'Smoothing' as you approach the current year will be found to be more accurate than following the 'peaks'.

Don't overdo the budgeting split-up to the stage where the pens and pencils must be accounted for.

Get every group head to budget for his area including, as well as capital and wages and salary expenditures:

๏ travel
๏ training
๏ office space
๏ transport: that part of the transport fleet costs that he spends

These can be on a rough split-up of company costs if not worth a full-scale computer split. This educates managers into cutting down office space and inefficient use of transport. (The cost of office space can be significant).

Engineers and scientists hate having to commit themselves to a budget for such 'frivolous' aspects of the job; but if you want an engineer to become a manager you will have to put him through this educational process.

Planning

Don't get on the bandwagon and plan for the sake of planning.

Plans have to be linked to the main objectives of your group. If you don't set these objectives, and set off on a plan-setting merry-go-round, the whole exercise will become a joke, rather like a game of Monopoly.

Never set plans from the top down without obtaining the active commitment of your subordinates to them by involvement in their formation.

'Never set plans from the top down . . . '

You'll get this commitment by inviting suggestions from junior management up; add your own and meet together to agree a final plan. If the plans are drawn up without such agreement then it would be better to file them in the waste-paper basket.

Set a scheme of plans that are linked from the top to the lowest group.

Pick the Pareto that will make the biggest difference to performance in the coming years; this should include three or so main measured parameters of each group, to watch how they fare; include these even for a group with a performance outstripping international competition—

remember it may run down leaving a gaping hole in your system.

Schedule work back from completion date (not forward from beginning date) and build in specific allowances for strikes and other contingencies; remember that when all your plans are correctly drawn up reality can only be worse than that. The strikes allowance should vary with the location (urban and rural are very different); the contingencies should vary with who is handling the job (old reliable hand or new untried) and which contractors (if any) are on it.

Attitude-shaping

Think of the capable people you know: they all have one fine quality—composure. They are confident that they know what they are doing—and they do know.

The advice given by Australian John Landy to a young Irish miler (Ron Delaney) is sound advice for us all: relax! Don't fight against it, breath regularly, don't use energy slowing yourself down. Delaney had quality but he was trying so hard he was tired before a race was half over. He subsequently won the 1500 m Olympic race with his friend Landy on his heels. Landy had injured his foot the previous day, never said a word about it, and was first to congratulate Delaney.

This incident has a moral for attitudes to colleagues at work. Be friendly. Help them if you can. Life is not such a rat race that you cannot take pleasure watching a pal win. If you've helped him you will be the more pleased to congratulate him.

Relaxed, you are in control of a situation. You have the main objectives in mind. Bumping, boring, passing, or boxing in will not panic you. If you happen to have red hair, colleagues may of course expect you to be a bit more fiery.

Don't spend too much of your time with subordinates who work near you. This gives remoter staff the impression that your inner court is the place for favourite sons. Indeed this 'inner court' is often comprised of *thinkers* who are not involved in the part of a business that makes or breaks it.

Don't trust anyone who calls you 'Sir'; it is not warranted. Remember beggars whose 'Sirs' are followed by flowery curses when alms are not forthcoming. Did you ever notice how polite the driving licence tester is? Or the detective or tax collector? They are polite not because you deserve it but because it suits their purpose.

Never forget that youth sees older men as:

❍ hidebound and hiding behind red tape
❍ lacking in initiative
❍ having shipped oars awaiting retirement
❍ schoolteachers spotting and gloating over mis-spellings, but not involved themselves in essay-writing

You've met the egoist who regularly criticizes everyone—'I never thought much of:

❍ General de Gaulle
❍ Willy Brandt
❍ John F. Kennedy
❍ Winston Churchill
❍ You (when you are not listening)'

He's just trying to equate himself with such people by looking down on them. If he recognizes and accepts how clever and able they are he widens the gap.

If you discover that a colleague has lied to you, record it and send him a copy. He'll claim that your record is untrue, so challenge him (in writing) to say what had occurred. Silence will follow.

Think twice—be nice

Be very slow to score off people; it is too easy. You know the type who excuses his insulting remarks, his vicious attacks, his bad-tempered outbursts, by professing that he is honest and 'says what he thinks'; he is not a cunning, plotting, prevaricating schemer like the rest of us. It would be interesting to lock up a half-dozen of these specimens in a room for a day.

Be kind to your assistants. Remember one of them may one day be your boss. Rugby clubs allow men at their peak to get on the first team and they regard it as no disgrace to go back down to the fourth as they get older and pass their peak. Be kind to those you meet on the way up—remember you will meet them on the way down again.

Remember no one is so perfect that he has no oddities or Achilles' heel or oversensitivities; you will occasionally be surprised by this, but let it be. With patience and memory you may be able to avoid some difficult situations, but it is better to plan as if you were dealing with persons of perfection. After all, you don't realize your own oddities—if you did you would alter your style.

You may be proud of something you have done, but you may have cribbed it or got the right answer by incorrect methods. You may be pleased in the same way as a dog that catches a rabbit—pleased he made no mistakes this time: don't be *over*-proud of anything you have personally done.

Act the devil's advocate before talking in public, going on television, etc. Get a friend to try to tear you to pieces. Do the same before going to a Conciliation Court. You will find that only 75 per cent of the potential attack will evolve and you're on an easy wicket.

Cardinal rules of Chapter 3

DO	DON'T
● instigate something every day	● waste more than three months on any idea unless you have considerable support
● let instigator of ideas have his head	
● confine yourself to what can only be done by you	● leave a disease to fester
	● delay decisions
● put your cards face up on the table	● make excuses
	● bluff
● get all your facts right first time	● deflect from the target
	● open up a problem beyond the least possible
● have at hand records of important paramaters of your job	● become a glorified public relations officer
● budget well	● make arbitrary decisions
● set main objectives for your group	● have *ad hoc* unlinked plans
● be composed	● score off others

4. *Your part in the pyramid*

The people you work with

Tell your colleagues about their mistakes, not by being smart about it or writing to them formally; just tip them off. They will do the same for you and you need not spend time eliminating the last vestiges of possibility of unimportant error from your efforts. This way you and your colleagues will be more effective as a bunch. It's not the absence of small errors, but the mass of effective, practical, and economic, improvements you can achieve that counts. If you were infallible you certainly would not be, at your age, in the post you now hold.

Don't be critical of other departments. You know the man whose conversation runs:

- ➋ 'That "shower" in Personnel'
- ➋ 'I've told that lot a dozen times'

Everyone is out of step except Johnny.

Don't believe that your image or reputation or infallibility must not be dented; you'll never complete the course—some bumping is inevitable. If you try to row from Dublin to Liverpool without getting wet you'll never get beyond the mouth of the Liffey.

If something ambiguous or erroneous comes to you from a colleague don't be smart and think you'll have a wonderful jeer at his expense. 'Ah—but you fellows don't know what you're doing. I've got two separate requests—one for three electricians and one for five electricians—what do you expect me to do?'

Come off it—be a help—find out which is right and do it at once.

Always leave an escape for any contestant—like a 'spot the deliberate error' contest. If you don't leave an exit you may corner a rat who will fight for his life.

If you have to lean very heavily on someone, but then see him being successful in a job unconnected with your bailiwick—congratulate him. He will appreciate that you may admire his work in one area but will still push him into giving the service you need. Your job may be something he just doesn't like doing.

Leave tasks to those who should do them. If they mess a job up, tell them what was wrong. If they mess it up a second time do it yourself and say not a word. When they find out, they will be hopping mad and will fire alarm rockets in all directions. Sit tight, say nothing and if they get on their bicycles and have it done before you start the third time let them have the job back, but not otherwise.

If they insist, via your boss, that you should not interfere, write a *mea culpa* note, but when the need arises repeat the treatment. *Mea culpa* notes cost little to write and allow you to get the job done. Your boss should be well pleased, having noted that you apologized and at the same time got the job done. One or two such efforts and your colleagues will get that much more efficient as they fear losing their job.

The importance of alibis

Keep a written record of all agreements with (and send it to) the manager who leaves everything vague and fluid and reneges when the pressure is on. As you reach an agreement on the 'phone, be writing: 'agreed—you will send me so and so by next week' and pop it in the tray for typing as the pleasantries of signing off are in progress.

Don't bother writing to the man who always keeps his word on agreements made. Just jot down on your drawing or file what was agreed (in case you are away and someone wants to know the score).

If anyone quotes an authority higher than you as the reason for non-action—be suspicious; higher authority may not know what you know. So find out! Having learned that this dodge won't work, the culprit won't try it on you again (although he probably will on others).

Never trust 'it is company policy'. On what basis did the Company decide—if they ever saw the problem at all? Maybe someone thinks the large 'C' of Company or 'B' for Board will frighten you from probing further. No Board would consciously decide in favour of inefficiency, waste of resources, duplication of effort, or stupidity.

Areas of responsibility

Don't:

➋ spend your time on demarcation disputes with other managers
➋ patrol your section attacking interlopers.

You move in to work on someone else's ground, perhaps on an extension to a plant. Some managers will make life hell by raising ten objections to everything that even vaguely impinges on their province. Give any such objector a signed note certifying that the item of which he complains is entirely your idea and responsibility, and then bash ahead.

Don't unduly encroach on other managers' staff or province. If you choose someone for promotion, check with his boss first and you may find that he is up for promotion in any case, prefers where he is, and was only interested in your territory as a poor second.

Never prevent anyone doing something because it may fail and reflect on you. The person trying the development has probably studied it in depth and is prepared to have a go at the expense of his own reputation.

Get to know two or three clear-minded people off whom you can bounce ideas. They need not be from your own group, nor indeed need they be in your outfit at all. About 1 per cent of people have this invaluable truthful objectivity. When such a partnership is operating both ways, each seeking advice on occasions from the other, it is one of the most valuable assets to effective action.

Don't confuse the issue by technical gobbledegook

❷ of course the osmotic superfluity of the reverse component precludes the use of . . .

This is gamesmanship and just wastes time. If anyone professes to agree with you he is probably an ass. Someone is going to get the real reason and the more you prevaricate the more suspicion you generate, and the more people long to take you down a peg because you are so darned uppity with your jargon.

If you can't make a presentation clear to your colleagues, you don't know your subject, or you are hiding something to con them into one line of action.

Whenever someone else reverts to jargon in talking to you,

look out—*you* are on to something worthwhile and *he* is bristling.

Company structure

Examine the organization to see if any level is contributing little or nothing. Dead wood can result because of the incumbent(s) or because the job is of no importance. In either case don't try to protect the image of the post; expose it to rough weather so that it will be made to work, or the incumbent will get out. If you have the power, do away with the post. You may hurt the incumbent(s)— but you gain respect and credibility, because the staff all know when a manager or post is useless.

Study the operations of managers; if their sole contribution is checking the work of others and passing largely negative comment or delaying the work, then their job is a non-job. If you have authority levels somewhat as follows:

Level 'A'	Approves	£500 000
'B'	,,	£50 000
'C'	,,	£5 000
'D'	,,	£500

Look at the economies you could effect by eliminating entirely level 'C' (and you probably have four of *them* for every 'A'). All you have to do is change the rule on authority levels and 'C' is out of a job.

Have at least six and up to ten reporting to a manager; then he will be busy enough to keep his nose out of any individual area. If you have an operating manager with only one or two reporting to him, he won't be busy enough and will interfere, half run, or undo their jobs.

Never have an in-line, in-the-way, deputy; you will drive

him round the bend by trying to keep tabs on what goes on below him. Such an in-line deputy will do little all year, and go crazy with activity during your vacations. He is a batman for the rest of the year; a batman, if needed at all, should be the office boy and paid as such—not Deputy Manager. Did you ever hear a group of 'deputies' describing their jobs? They live their years out waiting to get the top job when they can at last *do* something.

Give all deputies a specific written area of responsibility, and keep clear of it. A good division is to leave operations and short-term work to your deputy and keep long-term work for yourself.

'Nobody should have two bosses.'

Nobody should have two bosses; a man will either back one horse only and serve one boss to the virtual exclusion of the other, or he will serve neither. When one boss looks for services the man will claim he is busy for the second— in effect he has opted out of an impossible situation.

Tasks requested by, or required to be done for, outsiders should be estimated in man-days and with target dates (with the agreement of both sections). This will eliminate · the cuckoo who never hatches eggs.

Trimming the fat

Watch proposed changes in organization—centralization or decentralization, delegation or standardization, or so-called productivity deals. It is often merely the spread of Parkinson's Law; more people added—none substracted, even though before the change many were purported to be wasting time.

Don't take the word of senior managers that everyone is busy and more staff needed. Give credibility to the person who has reduced staff in certain areas, but not to the one who has always pressed for increases.

Cut out posts which exist only to

❍ co-ordinate
❍ liaise
❍ co-operate

If the staff can't co-ordinate, liaise or co-operate without an intermediary, it's time they were straightened out.

Avoid amateur specialists, i.e. one who has not learned a skill the hard way, from bottom up. Putting 'PVC' on a door does not make the incumbent an expert on it.

If you need a specialist, have nobody reporting to him and pay him on a scale suited to the specific nature of his job. This will prevent him building an empire in an effort to 'up' his salary.

Don't make the mistake of having a 'Specialist' without a

full day's pressing problems. Having recorded everything on which he is expert, don't let him sit admiring his handiwork.

Don't have a military-type structure; everyone will fight to get more and more assistants. Armies had to have officers in reserve to provide continuity as warriors were mown down; someone had to issue orders to shove more fighters into the breach. This practice has grown up in business. Officers allow warriors to be mown down whenever battle is joined, claiming that their delegation is so good that they need not check every detail; it would be foolish to sack the officer if the warrior is not a good swordsman.

Before restructuring a group, consult everyone who will be in the new set-up; get them to write what they think would be the correct structure. About 95 per cent will pen what you want to do and this will stop the 5 per cent grumblers who support the *status quo*.

Making success easier

Never leave a dud for longer than 2 years in any post; if he is a dud for 2 years he is a dud for ever. His subordinates will keep up hopes of improvement for a year or so but disillusion and disinterest will set in and this will kill effort and initiative; their golf handicap will reduce as their energies are deflected off the job.

When a job is going to be worth more because of new responsibilities, but the incumbent is not competent to do it properly, retitle the job and put a new man in.

Never split a job and leave half with the incompetent; move him sideways and replace him. You or your predecessors made the error of putting him in the job so it's your task to take him out of it. Otherwise, you'll have frustrated staff having to work with Joe Incompetent until his retirement, and then maybe trouble with the Unions over replacing him.

Never organize or re-organize on a permanent basis to suit Joe the problem man. Everyone knows the problem and if you don't face it and put Joe where he rightfully belongs, you will kill initiative for a long time in that area. A poor golfer who plays a slow round in front of many aspiring low scorers can slow up a course for the whole morning. If you don't make it so that aspirants of better quality can 'go through', they will leave the course.

If your organization was there before you came along it's easy to opt out of:

- ❍ removing incompetents
- ❍ changing structures where wrong
- ❍ cutting off out-of-date and obsolete areas.

Admittedly, it's far easier when starting with a clean sheet.

Staff control and training

Produce standards for anything that has to be done regularly:

- ❍ specifications
- ❍ designs
- ❍ drawings

The production of standards eliminates the know-all boss who squirrels all sorts of information in his head, or in his drawer, waiting to pounce on an unfortunate unknowing, unsuspecting subordinate.

To prevent senior staff from perpetually passing caustic

comments on juniors' work, insist that operational manuals be prepared.

These manuals should record what to watch out for and past errors. Detail one person to produce each such manual. His draft should be submitted to selected managers with experience in the particular field for detailed comment. Then produce the final version.

Once this has been done for all aspects of the work, young recruits can operate with confidence. If a boss tries the game of 'we tried that in 1952 but it didn't work' the junior can quote from more accurate records.

This scheme may provide less fun for those who like starting a job from scratch, hoping to put their imprint on an accepted change, but it is a surer method of operation.

Don't keep adding staff without subtracting somewhere. You probably know of posts that are fossilized with officers that have ceased to contribute and have reached their level of incompetence. Why keep them and add more? Re-organize, but rub out some of these posts or make them die with their incumbent.

You may be tempted, now and then, to promote staff just to keep a pot from boiling over. This is a short-term solution, encourages repeat boiling, and discourages staff from having a go somewhere else and widening their horizons. The inclination of most of us is to stay put and hope to get more money doing the one job better and better. We should be encouraged to break out of the cocoon and fly by ourselves. Promising young men, remaining in a protected atmosphere, may never live up to the promise.

It's like training dogs; raise a fool of a dog that can't catch a rat if it ran over his paws and you'll never turn him into a ratter. But train a pup as a ratter from the start and

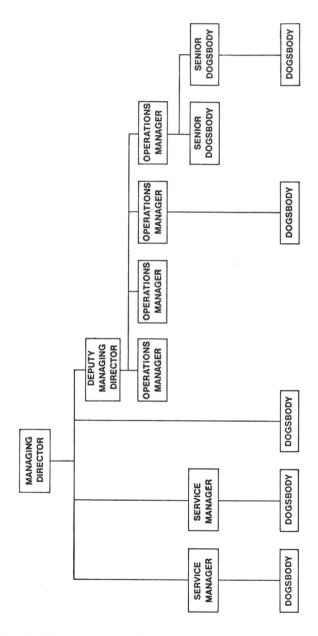

64 *To make life easier for yourself at work*

he will be valuable. It is better to have a few good ratters than a hundred fools.

Get policies set on anything you can and then avoid all the hundreds of specific cases relying on precedent.

Team-building

You have, no doubt, been handed the we-have-recommended-an-increase-in-staff-to-do-this-work-but-not having-got-it-how-can-management-expect-work-done argument. Thus, to do nothing, all that's necessary is keep pressing for more and more staff.

There is no optimum or correct number in any team; it is all a matter of judgement. With *less* people than previously, you have to make decisions faster with fewer facts, and with greater risk of missing the optimum solution and missing improvements. With more people than previously, you run the risk of underemploying your staff.

Our-establishment-has-not-been-filled-in-the-past-five-years-how-can-we-be-expected-to-produce-results, simply indicates that the establishment should be cut back.

Consider a group where initiating does not exist at senior levels. Ten per cent of the work goes up to the next manager in line and 10 per cent of *that* amount is returned for alteration; if both percentages were reduced to 1 per cent you could do without three managers, i.e. 20 per cent less.

Every man in a routine production job should have a fall-back project so that he can use his talents and experience to improve and develop his area of activity. This is a bonus to the company. These projects help him to prove his worth over and above running his routine job well; but watch that his primary job gets priority.

Use every skill available; if you are scared of letting an

'Use every skill available.'

accountant or actuary or engineer pry into your field, then you don't deserve to last. If you have the qualities required for the job, nobody can oust you. If you use experts fully your whole field benefits.

Don't leave bored qualified engineers doing a job that has been fully developed to the stage where technicians can run it.

Cardinal rules of Chapter 4

DO	DON'T
◑ help your colleagues	◑ be critical of colleagues
◑ leave an escape for a contestant	◑ try to leave your image undented
◑ generate a few friends who objectively help you	◑ bother with demarcations
◑ eliminate any post no longer required	◑ have in-line deputies
◑ have 6 to 10 reporting to each group boss	◑ have any posts for co-ordinating others
◑ get standards set for everything	◑ have specialists with no set problems and dates
	◑ promote anyone to keep a group happy

5. *The man at the top*

Communicate upwards properly. Keep your boss in the picture on what he should know (1 per cent of what you are at) *and no more*. A good manager has this gift. I wonder why? Because he communicates those items likely to impact on the boss through reaction from outside his territory.

Always terminate any discussion with your boss before he does. In this way you won't need to be 'dismissed' and you will not obviously waste his time or take up too large a slice of it. It may sound impressive to say you were no less than 2 hours with old T.J. but what did he think? Probably that you are trying to impress him with the complexity of your job and that you are unfit to run the show.

Alter on the spot anything sent back for unimportant alterations by your boss. Have it back to him in 15 minutes or trivial alterations will appear to be of greater significance. The speed of turnaround will indicate the irrelevance of the change and prevent the irrelevance irritating you.

If something is wrong and you know it, set it right and see that your boss knows of it. It is no excuse that someone between you and the boss wants a quiet life.

'Oh yes,' he will say, 'Bert said something about that to me and I was expecting the facts from him but as he dropped it I took it that he was satisfied everything was O.K.'

Remember that when the bubble bursts you're the one who'll carry the blame. Don't give up when you are dead right (your esteemed colleagues agree). This exercise could be termed 'putting manners on the boss'. He'll respect the subordinate who fights his corner and produces facts to enable the company to change course when off beam.

'Let your boss think your bright ideas are his own—if he is the type who operates thus.'

Bosses good and bad

If *you* can't get done what should be done, but it is approved further up the line, your influence and effort will be seen as poor by your subordinates. Let your boss think your bright ideas are his own—if he is the type who operates thus——but make sure he is the only one who thinks this is so.

A good test of a good boss is—would you take it to heart if he severely rebuked you? If your boss is peevish or bad-tempered this will not worry you. But if he is fair, honest, composed, helpful, and able, then you should and would take it to heart if he reprimanded you.

In your youth get working for a boss who has quality. Don't stay working for a boss who is incompetent. You will spend far too much time making allowances for his ineptitude, checking on what he does, following up useless queries. You are a member of a losing team. Get away horizontally.

Nor should you stay working for a boss who is unhelpful. You will learn nothing; you will have to act as if he did not exist; you cannot approach him with a problem in its half-warmed condition to pick his brains.

Get working for a boss who keeps you at stretch and imparts knowledge to you, tries you out and loads you up with worthwhile work. You have but one youth to live and you must learn as efficiently as you can.

Cardinal rules of Chapter 5

DO	DON'T
❷ pick a good boss	❷ waste his time
❷ keep him informed	❷ give up if you are right but the boss objects
	❷ stay working for an incompetent

6. *Of carrots and sticks*

Practical recruitment guidelines

Pre-test under-graduates by giving them a vacation project, one for each, to discover before you employ any of them

- ❍ can they think out what a problem is and work to a conclusion (positive or negative)
- ❍ do they work hard
- ❍ can they pull with people

Don't judge on bulk, hair or clothing. Young persons who dress as the previous generation did are doing so just for the interview. Or they are naturally dull.

Take on some men who have been around a bit and found out that drab green of those far-away hills. They will help to counteract starry-eyed youngsters taking off for greener pastures.

Take on some with outside experience not available in the company; this will improve techniques and save employing consultants.

No bluff please. Why advertise that the firm has 'wonderful promotional opportunities' unless it is expanding into a new field or with a new product? You are setting yourself up for a load of disgruntled employees—unless of course you have a plan to shoot two or three fairly senior managers monthly. Leave it to the applicant to decide *on facts*

'Dont judge on bulk, hair, or clothing.'

whether he wants to join. Advertising for a middle management position 'wonderful promotional opportunities' is
mighty insulting to existing staff, who also read the newspapers.

Never overpay to recruit; if that's all you have to offer the
bees will leave the honey as soon as they find a more
interesting job.

Performance assessment

Watch out for good judgement—it is rare, and does not

come in recognizable packages. If a man's work is always right, cherish him. He has outstandingly good judgement and not just good luck. A particularly good test would be the number of times you have opposed him and then found him to be right. He is no sycophant. He is helping the company to reach better decisions.

Watch out for the man who always emerges from the ruck with the ball. Others are holding jerseys, hacking shins, facing the wrong way, shouting for a pass. It's a sense of positioning and timing, and keeping an eye on the ball—and it's also a spark of genius. You can't educate or train anyone to gain the spark of genius of a Pelé or a Muhammad Ali any more than an Einstein, a Churchill, or a Barnes Wallis.

Study your subordinates to see if any of them like the job they are doing so much that they isolate it with an iron curtain from the scrutiny of top management. You may find they are not really able to cope with the job they have, let alone take on something more difficult further up the line.

There are some who excel once tasks are set down for them; slightly better performers begin to set their own tasks once they are put through the exercise a few times; the best of all are those who set their own proper tasks right from the start.

Don't spend time protecting managers who are not pulling their weight. To get results, ineffective, useless, or shifty managers must be exposed. Visit them without notice occasionally when they are working with their subordinates to see how the game is being played.

You can spend a lot of time upholding the authority of all managers at all costs, or you can encourage everyone from junior to senior rank to work effectively to forward the aims of the company. Those who deserve encouragement from you, whatever their rank, are those who

- ◑ work hard
- ◑ are effective
- ◑ are honest

and this goes also for those not reporting directly to you.

It is not good management to side against subordinates with experts from outside your department.

An engineering production manager, for instance, fearing strange disciplines, taking the safe line that the experts must surely be right and without the knowledge or mettle to debate a question with them, may take sides with design, finance, personnel, sales, or public relations people against his own subordinates. He is more concerned with appeasing his horizontal colleagues than with being a good manager, trusted and respected by his staff. There will be occasions when he has to rule in favour of outside agencies, but when a subordinate puts the issue to him it will have to be thrashed out pretty thoroughly if it is not to have serious repercussions on production.

Spotting the losers

If a manager makes one serious error of judgement—warn him. If he makes three, withdraw from him authority on matters of serious import. If you are managing effectively, not more than one per cent of your staff should need such treatment.

Remember—it's only those who are regularly late arriving who will object to a check on timekeeping. They'll prob- · ably stress the obvious truth that, in their job, performance can't be measured by minutes spent in the office. But the example to junior staff engaged on routine work can be disastrous.

Watch carefully those who continually claim that they are

'busy'. If anyone claims he is always 100 per cent occupied he should not get any further; correction—he should probably not be in his present job. His 'busyness' means that he never has time to improve the job, or to make a case for and battle to get improvements made.

If all those claiming to be 'overloaded' would just shut up moaning about it for a month—think of the vacuum that would be formed; a vacuum that could be filled with useful work. Think of the increased productivity!

It's a pleasure to work with managers who dig in without continual reference to

❍ workload
❍ staff shortage
❍ idle assistants

You know you'll get from them the right answer to any query in five minutes. It's no such pleasure to deal with the performer who has the most reasonable and complex reasons for doing nothing:

❍ the insurance aspects of night travel in the USSR
❍ the responsibility of the contractor for insurance between fob and quay

This is obstruction; shooting off queries which he should have checked beforehand instead of raising genuine problems.

Distrust anyone who says he will do a simple job in two months' time. What does he think he's being asked to do—design the first rocket to Jupiter? It means that he dislikes the job, does not know what to do, is aghast at the complexity of the task, wants to lend it an inordinate air of importance, and is not going to do it.

Have you had the galling experience of being asked to 'ring me in the morning to remind me' or 'get your Secretary to ring me'? He'd better be the only person who can supply the goods, or drop him fast.

Is anyone always on the 'phone when you try to contact him? Or, worse still, on both (or all three) 'phones. This is the carrying-this-place-on-my-back syndrome.

When to promote

The selection of those for promotion is mighty important to you in your job, and to how you yourself will be able to perform.

Promote on results. There is no substitute. All the better if you don't particularly like the guy or if you never meet socially. If he is clearly identifiable as the one who produces the goods—up he goes. A sure test is one who moves into a division where losses are piling up, and turns it around. Put him in charge of the biggest division you have.

Promote the person who has proven his ability in those aspects that are more prominent in the higher position. The 'Peter Principle' may apply if you make your best fitter a supervisor; but not if you make into a supervisor the good fitter who is a dab hand at handling staff and planning work.

Don't promote a man in the hope that he may match the task, or on the argument that he was not bad where he is but maybe a change will show his merit. A loser is always a loser, once he has been truly tried out in a position of responsibility.

An employee who can initiate and instigate has potential. He could be instigating things that are supposed to be his boss's province. Promote the man who has ideas to lift the job forward a decade and prove it to you with facts and figures.

Who to promote

Be careful not to tend to select people of your style or temperament. Often, the interaction of two different temperaments will benefit both parties. To guard against this, use formal assessments as a yardstick for choices.

If you pick a weak person for promotion for

- the sake of peace
- because he is 'in line' for it
- because he happens to be in your own section
- to keep up hope in the area from which he is drawn
- because you can't promote too many from one group and must thus take the best from another

you may finish up having a weak link in the chain; you now have to get the work done by

- forcing the weak man to keep up pace
- hoping his subordinates will do so
- doing the work yourself

You'd probably have been better off not filling the job at all.

Promote mental heavyweights. Lightweights get blown about with a stiff breeze. This assumes you don't want to run a one-man show with yes-men support.

Heavyweights

- are always on time
- do not make excuses

- ◑ do not let you delay
- ◑ look like potentials to take on your job
- ◑ are right in practice—even when you had grave doubts.

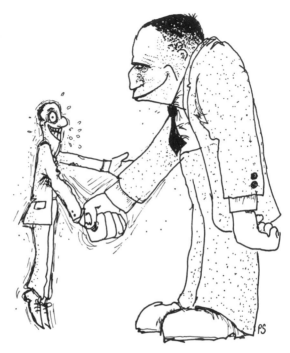

'Promote heavyweights.'

If you have an organization where intelligent, able persons are bottled up by dull bluffers you will have an unhappy poor-output company. I assume for the sake of this argument that the Managing Director has top ability; if not, you had better get out. Of course, if you are dull yourself you won't see any of this going on.

Don't promote the man who is deferential; he is impressed with *you*, and goodness knows why he should be, or he is impressed with the furniture and fittings in your office, or with the post. Sycophants are two-faced—they flatter a boss and whip subordinates.

Avoid putting a kingfisher* into a planning job. Get the man who is not afraid to consider ALL the pros and cons—even if he loses power by the result. Otherwise your forward planning will consist of justification of past practices (handled by the kingfisher) and demarcation disputes with other departments.

Promote nine out of ten on merit and leave the tenth to allow an older man to reach his peak. If you don't, the low flyer will never get to his peak and you break his spirit. Any organization should have a reasonable distribution of persons by age and ability.

In selecting for promotion watch for danger signs in the make-up of the contenders:

- the man who talks non-stop, never listening to anyone else; he thinks he learned it all before you had the luck to acquire him
- the fellow who can't hold his drink—even off the job; it's dangerous
- the one who follows you into more than one club—it may be a coincidence but consider whether it is
- persons who have no (or poor) sense of humour. They gather others of similar type around them and form a group that is hurt or offended by everything

There is nothing wrong with a man in a middle level job who is excellent in the post and never gets higher. The genius in selection is to have each man stop where he is on top of his job—and no higher.

* The kingfisher allows no other on his stretch of river

The team

Having those who are friendly and co-operative with each other is the greatest guarantee of success. How do you get it? Perhaps your predecessor left it to you. It's not the man who laughs most but the one with humour and integrity that you want. Integrity can be seen in the one who criticizes his own efforts, and changes immediately a colleague offers a better solution—no ifs and buts, no justification, no prevarication.

Work hard to obtain a friendly, helpful, encouraging, stimulating atmosphere: avoid strenuously a repressive, authoritarian atmosphere.

Be prepared to bend your organization to suit any real talent you have. Good men, outstanding men, are rare so don't hem them in with too little scope. But be careful not to land yourself in trouble when a good man leaves (or dies); don't fill his post unless you have another just as good.

Good men are referred to affectionately by subordinates as The Boss; despised bosses are referred to as HE.

Poor performers appear at any age; some fizzle out at 20, others at 40.

On this question of poor performers there is an important distinction. If you have a young man of no promise advise him to look for a job elsewhere. If you have a man at lower middle management level and 40 years of age you have a problem; he cannot easily get a job elsewhere and your company policy may well be not to edge out such persons. If he is still capable of doing a day's work at the decision level of a young man, put him out of the main stream and give him such responsibilities.

Most difficult of all problems is the manager near the top who only then is found sadly lacking. You will have to give him some high sounding title and move him sideways where he cannot do any harm. The nearer the top the more dangerous is this disease as it affects other people right down the line.

Always give a poor performer a severe definite warning with a deadline for improvement before taking action.

Don't employ only people who have what you see as a 100 per cent chance of getting right to the top. Ideally what you want is one person certain to get to the top in every generation (at age 40–45) and one certain to fill every other senior post as it becomes vacant. To be sure of doing this successfully a crop of no more than three times the finally required number should be entered in the race. Otherwise you will have a company of disgruntled primadonnas.

Never advise a subordinate to take any particular post; if he is a failure he will blame it on you and not on himself. You may have advised an erstwhile colleague who is now a subordinate to take a job where he has fossilized—well you can't win every time!

NEVER NEVER NEVER promise anything in the way of salary increase, promotion, prospects, fringe benefits, power or extra responsibilities before you have approval to do so.

Even if you are sure or certain or positive; even if you have it in writing that such would be normal; even if you trod the same path twenty times and found no problems. You raise hopes which may have to be dented or dashed and even if somewhat later you fulfil the promise your word is effectively broken.

It is far better to leave staff with unconfirmed hopes which, if realized, give satisfaction. Do not seek the personal gratification of buttering Joe up with an early promise. All you're doing is getting pleasure by promising something that will be welcomed. You are not in the game for the personal gratification.

Using the interview

Always ask specific questions, and get quantification for everything

- ◗ did you publish it? Can I read a copy?
- ◗ What date was the project completed? What was the planned date?

Don't talk for more than 5 per cent of the interview. If you talk for 20 per cent of the time you are simply trying to prove how smart you are to the unfortunate interviewee and your colleague interviewer who is probably your boss.

Don't be chatty with the interviewee about his family or his sports interests; some interviews contain little else. Find all this out at the annual staff party.

Never pick staff for promotion solely as a result of a 20-minute interview. You'll be fooling yourself since you can't know

- ◗ if he is co-operative
- ◗ if he is productive
- ◗ if his judgement can be crazy on a particular topic.

Use assessments for everyone in the company. (See 'Staff appraisal', p. 91). Without them to back up an interview it is difficult to pick the best; it may mean that the *older* applicant has the better chance for success, and not necessarily the *best* applicant.

Try not to believe that anyone from outside your own staff is the better candidate; this is the green on the faraway hills. It's amazing how well-groomed, well-dressed, well-spoken, erudite, and knowledgeable some perfectly useless performers can appear in a short interview.

Use a long interview and prepare precise questions for those who come from outside your company. Make it as thorough as you can. Check with someone in the interviewee's present company if you can; this is worth a day's interviewing. I've seen some ghastly blunders in over- and under-estimation of the abilities of strangers.

Praise and blame

Don't be too proud to congratulate—we know how critical you can be. It is harder to praise than blame. It lowers the differential between you and the recipient and perhaps you fear the narrowing (or reverse) gap.

Everyone thinks he is doing (within the limitations set on him by the organization and his boss) a pretty capable job. He doesn't understand why no whisper of praise rewards his daily efforts. He never sees himself as lacking in judgement, or being precipitous, or stupid. . . . Then, having had no praise for 51 weeks of serious concentrated effective effort, he gets a rocket from management.

Each boss should make it his business to know important moves his immediate subordinates have made so that he can comment and offer praise. As a manager I am constantly coming across excellent work done some time back that was not even brought to my attention at the time— not from modesty but because there is no ready way by which a subordinate can, without appearing to brag, keep you informed. Once you have established a bank of knowledge and can acknowledge excellence, you are in a good position when you need to criticize adversely the one item in 10 000 that goes awry.

Ring or, better still, write (he can show his pals) a congratulatory note to someone who sets you back on your heels:

To: Well Done
Subject: *Budgets*
      Excellent

               signed: I.M. Pressed

Watch for the manager who continually blames and criticizes his subordinates, particularly where you don't see the faults when he is absent, and didn't see them before he moved in. He is using criticism of others as the reason for his own inefficiency:

❷ I haven't received the figures from x
❷ As usual, y gave me a load of rubbish

When did he ask for the information—on time, or five minutes ago?

The good manager *always* praises his staff, supporting them before his colleagues and his boss; this shows that a team is working well.

Don't NAG. Nagging is:

❷ continually questioning
   why didn't you?
   where is . . . ?
   didn't I already tell you?
❷ never offering help
❷ invariably giving negative decisions—from a sense of righteousness as if all others were Publicans and you the Pharisee
❷ being irritable; better see a doctor

⊙ never seeing anything well done (or even fairly well done); only seeing what is still to be done
⊙ never giving unstinted praise; always a sting in it
⊙ I-can't-turn-my-back-for-a-minute-around-here

Did you ever see an old hatching hen with newly-hatched helpless chicks—squak, squak, squak, cluck, cluck, cluck. Can your chicks raise a peep?

Treating the troops right

When you talk to staff below the rank of the manager reporting directly to you, ask questions but do not make decisions overriding the opinions of the manager; wait until you leave the scene and then tackle the manager to see if he can justify his line of action. It's OK to tease out all aspects by asking questions: 'Did you investigate having three outlets . . .?'

If you don't adopt this attitude you won't obtain the loyalty of the manager. Your visits will appear to him as designed to make an ass of him in front of his own staff.

How long should you wait before you lower the boom on a poor performer? Have patience even when you feel irritated or justified in blowing your top. You should give plenty of warning and opportunity to recover. Give every chance to co-operate, to see the light. Amend your requirements slightly and try again *but* if all fails lower the boom. If you don't have the guts to do so the staff will be only too well aware that you chickened out.

Ask your subordinates what, in their opinion, *you* are not doing that you should be doing. Having done so, work on it, thus strengthening your hand to get them to react favourably to your similar criticisms. Don't argue over any of their comments—that is merely trying to prove you are really perfect. It is useful to select three managers (one young and independent, one middle aged and competent, one older, reliable and outspoken) and ask in writing for their frank comments. If they do not trust you you will get nothing worthwhile. Would it surprise you if all three listed the same item first without knowing the other two had also been asked? This happened to me and should really not have been such a surprise; it just meant that it sure was first.

Remember that nobody understands intelligence superior to his own; consider the number of people that you regard as slow-witted and muddled, versus the number that you know can out-think you; then pause and reflect, are you really God? Having concluded that you are certainly not, realize that superior intelligence cannot be properly appreciated; if it could you would have it!

Make it clear that you are perfectly aware that someone is not delivering the goods.

'You put a date of 1 March last on production of x. Since then I've enquired monthly and now would like your written explanation as to why this assignment is so late.'

Monthly enquiries of this sort can be carried out by your secretary without direction (out of your BF file, into which she puts the query in the first place—again without direction).

Never be sarcastic at subordinates' expense—particularly with anyone else listening; it's too easy and too hurtful. Think how you'd feel if the roles were reversed.

Neither should you criticize a manager's work in the presence of one of his colleagues or one of his subordinates —you would rightly lose his loyalty.

'Mol an oige is tioci si' is an old Gaelic proverb; it means praise the young and they will react favourably. Try it on young and old alike.

Human problems

Seek the reason why Willy is not pulling his weight. It may be problems off the job: illness he is trying to conceal in case it tells against him, financial worries due to family illness, incompatibility with his boss or a poor boss. Watch the boss who throws up more than one incompatible subordinate.

Remember that a man with a nagging wife will be irritable and aggressive at work.

Be slow to believe that anyone is malingering. The pride and dignity of a man depend partly on his satisfaction in doing a task well. He will not purposely do it badly. He may not have the ability; he may have gone down in intelligence; he may be ill, even mentally ill, but plain malingering is rare.

Avoid having incompatibles working together. You will find this out in your annual chats. It's not good enough to leave such a situation to work itself out. You would be better to leave several posts unfilled than have incompatibles together. Incompatibles spend all their time scoring off others. If one is old and the other young you may find the older one is bullying a man with more ability.

Result-getting tactics

Give each man in each post, whether functional or not, a specific task and date for completion. The date should be set by the man himself, and agreed by you.

Allow a reasonable, but specified time for the answer to queries or the supply of data. If not received by the due data, do it yourself or have it done by someone else, and let the original man see the answer. Let everyone know that this is the ruling. But you had better answer everything that reaches you well within the deadline!

These rules should apply to you and all your staff in their dealing with other departments and companies. No routine acknowledgements should be issued. This just means the query is being put aside to be dealt with later, probably much later.

Always specify the exact date by which you want results. But be fair: if everyone knows you must submit budgets on 16 March, don't ask for them on 16 February from your subordinates. They have to work them out—you only have to vet them.

Don't accept excuses for lack of results: 'All these people were foisted on me when I took over the job. If I could hand-pick my own people, I'd make this place hum. I'm no manager—a real manager must be able to hire and fire his staff'.

In other words, he could only captain a football team entirely selected by himself—not by the team manager. This is the canonization complex. He's the saint and his colleagues and predecessors sinners.

Never jump authority lines by asking one person to do a job and then chatting up his assistant about it. Nobody knows now who is responsible for getting it done and remember if it's a 51:49 sort of decision everyone will be afraid to finalize it. You will not gain the trust of subordinates.

When you want a quick approximate answer make it clear: 'give me to the nearest £50 000 by Wednesday 14th what you will spend by the end of the year'.

This prevents the detail chaser from taking up too much of his time giving you an answer of a total expenditure of

£64 267·42 which is of no interest to you when you are trying to ascertain whether total costs will be close to £14 000 000 for the year. It also prevents follow-up calls or notes amending it to £64 268·31. Remember there is an accountant producing costs at the other end and to him any digit incorrect is a sin which he will correct.

Challenge managers to produce in writing the MAIN improvements they see must be undertaken—only those worth 1 per cent of the turnover of their department are worthwhile. If no suggestions then the manager is no good. The most convincing ones advocate a reduction of control over resources by the manager concerned.

Help subordinates to reach their goals; ask if can you help in any way—but theirs is the goal and the credit. If you want any improvement or alteration in their work be specific and give the exact reasons.

If you want action, do something which will amuse or set the 'phones and voices going. Try a memo consisting of just a question mark '?'; or sending an unsigned memo with 'you would not care to get such a rude insulting comment' on the margin.

Personal diplomacy

Don't use a condescending or dictatorial tone: 'this is a very complex matter that takes months to calculate'— implying that you need to be very clever or highly educated to understand it.

Don't act offended: 'I don't do all this work for fun'— implying that nobody is entitled to query it.

In an argument, don't peevishly throw down your pencil or glasses on the table. Unfortunately such traits are largely habitual so what can one do about them? Modify them to the best of one's ability.

Remember, there is a world of difference between being efficient and being unfair or rude. No one admires either the inefficient or the rude.

Only talk in terms of facts

- 15 hours
- £276·49
- I will answer that today
- I will get Joe's opinion by 10.00 hours
- Jack—can you get the enquiry out by Tuesday?

Realize that in common with every other manager you think that:

- you don't get your fair share of the company budget
- you don't have enough staff (look at your unfilled positions, 2 sick, 3 on vacation)
- you are not allowed to offer sufficient pay to attract staff
- you have a tougher job than most (I said you *think* you have!)

You must meet deadlines without recourse to such excuses —in emergency conditions you might even have to do some work yourself! 'Better late than never' is out; 'Late is never' is the rule.

Never lose your rag. On occasions be 'professionally' aggressive or annoyed; put on a show of being so to get results; but if you are not calm at the back of the show it will be bad temper.

If you are bad-tempered, eventually your colleagues will tire of it and stop making allowances; they won't bother telling you so but you will be ostracized (redheads are faster on the draw than others and need to try harder on this front). Neither should you be constantly aggressive. (People of small stature are often so; bulky persons are not).

Build up a Relay Team to get things done, leaving out anyone who has more than once prevaricated or failed to meet a deadline: those on 'B', 'C', and 'D' teams will never form part of the record-breaking 'A' team. A trusted member of this team would deliver the goods in writing with two minutes to go even if he flew in from Tokyo half-an-hour before.

Confine yourself to making the errors *you* should be making instead of making those that should be made by your subordinates!

Staff appraisal

Make a formal appraisal of staff yearly; if anyone is scored below the acceptable level find out by discussion with him:

- how he rates himself
- where the discrepancy (if any) is when compared with the official result; often there is none
- reasons for discrepancy? The following two cases were enlightening:
  (a) Man scored low on bossing subordinates and OK on getting on with colleagues and boss. He scored himself OK on the first but bad on the second.
      Reason: he was more intelligent than his bosses but had no chance (lack of education) that he saw of passing them out; had fun tripping them up.
      Result: saw the joke and stopped it.
  (b) Man scored low on dealing with subordinates; scored himself OK, reasoning that he made sure any

error they made was discussed with them in detail so that they would never welsh on him. Changed horizontally when he realized the nonsense of his attitude and the problem disappeared.

No boss you ever had was a puzzle to you; you could have given an A1 assessment of him to top management, but you never got the chance. It is death to a company if the bluffers, the lazy, the chancers begin to float to the top because top managers do not know the score. Install an upsidedown assessment scheme to allow junior managers to assess their seniors. As a senior manager yourself, listen carefully to individual workers to find out the score on other managers.

Don't show assessments to staff concerned or the managers assessing them will under-play their ratings. A young man who knows he's been rated 9, 9, 10, 8, 9, 9 is likely to get a swollen head and be ruined. Be happy to promote him and hope he keeps it up. However, let staff know if they are rated below average on any one aspect of their job, and give them the chance to discuss it.

Don't include character traits in the scheme or, if you do, certainly do not discuss them with the men concerned. 'Judgement', for example. Judging judgement is subjective and risky. Keep to job performance. If judgement is bad it will show up here.

Design an assessment form for each specific job category. Don't use one for the whole company to cover salesmen and research chemists. It will be so general as to be useless.

Use more than three categories of performance. 'Bad', 'average', 'excellent' means that most people will be placed in the middle grade.

Judge how good managers are at sizing up staff by the

assessments they submit. One may grade all his subordinates as 'excellent', another grade all his as 'average'. This simply means that neither of them can judge performance accurately.

Advise poor performers engaged in a specific task that they are in a job requiring good performance and to look around for a move within or without the company.

Assessments by two separate managers may not concur, but they present a clear picture. It should show if a man is in the wrong job; if he is OK for the job; if he is shaping up to be outstanding or poor.

Financial reward

See that your staff's pay is right for the job they do and don't settle for anything less.

Don't just act as commentator on genuine staff claims for pay as they pass up and down your level in the organization. Make up your mind what is right, take off your coat and go after it.

Management courses

Send men of good judgement on top management courses— it will repay tenfold—they will be different and better men. Having a group of managers working together who have been on such courses is an advantage in that they are *au fait* with the management facilities and techniques available.

Don't send a man of poor judgement and narrow vision on a top level management course—he will lapse into a stupor in a week, but he will remember the jargon which he will trot out as proof that he is now top management potential.

In order to validate the integrity of the most complex interpersonal flux in facial confrontations circumscribed by cognitive parameters it becomes less important to adopt a modal approach the more the distribution of psycho-peripheral phenomena approximates to the hyperstasis experienced in zone- and non-zone activities of the phase of heightened alienation when as an alternative the factor analysis made in low-objective-orientation groups can be related to peaking on the low cusps of two or more syncopated sine-curves interfacing on congruent or quasi-congruent planes expressed in alpha-wave core patterns helically scanned in sequential but radically opposing frequencies dynamized by the generation of high/low and low/high decision capacities rationally held to deviate from the mean equivalence proposed in compound plateaux formed

PS

'He will lapse into a stupor, and trot out the jargon he remembers.'

Run in-company courses on

- effective speaking
- languages

immediately after normal working hours; this will eliminate those who would attend in working hours just for a change of scene.

Reading

Read Drucker, Parkinson and *Up the Organization* by

Robert Townsend, *The Peter Principle* by Dr L. J. Peter and R. Hull, *Management and Machiavelli* by Antony Jay, and go on from there.

Watch the shelves in managers' offices. It's a good pointer to a man's judgement to see which particular books he thought good. Take it as a rule of thumb that a man's skill in management is in inverse proportion to the number of such books *on display* in his office. They should be returned to the company library when he has read them, to be recalled again if necessary. He's not likely to read them again *in toto* and at most would need to refer to one chapter in two years' time. He believes they impress visitors behind the glass of his bookshelf.

Reading management books is largely an exercise in self-justification. The indifferent manager enjoyed *The Peter Principle* as much as the excellent manager. Both recognized others in it. Readers of management books (including this one!) nod their heads wisely as they browse, seeing themselves as the wise-balanced-far-seeing-sympathetic-super-communicating-efficient-hero. References to inefficiency-sloth-vacillation-lack-of-communication-poor style are clearly seen as the villainous others. Would you please realize that it may be *you* who is being described, but I'm taking no bets that you can or will do an iota about it.

Bone up on specific skills that are needed in your job:

- interviewing
- work study
- staff assessment schemes
- budgetary control
- computer programming
- Russian language
- job evaluation

◑ MBO (if you don't know what that means you are in a poor state).

You can get this knowledge from the literature gradually or in a series of formal courses but watch that you learn new skills that develop as the years pass.

The velvet glove

When inviting someone to your office say something like:

'Would you have a minute?'
'Are you busy there?'

and say what the problem is—budget, new machine . . . implying that you are looking for help.

Don't intimidate by

'Come down at 11.00' or
'Come down at once!'

It's bad for nerves (and ulcers). After all, they probably don't expect the news to be of the best.

Avoid a dictatorial, aggressive tone in discussion; if you do so your facts are suspect, or you would put them on the table for all to see the quality. Decisions are not to be made on the timbre but on the quality of the wave shape.

The iron fist

However, if a manager is not doing his job (= the results are not up to the set figures or on time) and defies you by making a joke of the whole thing, by ignoring you, or by calmly plodding along in first gear—then put your foot down. Everyone knows of this battle of wills and it's either you or he who will win. State firmly what is wrong and put a date on its total rectification or his dismissal. If he has any ability he will pull around.

Integrity

If you say something mean it and then do it.

Don't lie; if you do, it will snowball and a fantastic memory will be needed to extricate yourself. You'll be found out and you have now given everyone else the perfect right to lie to you.

Never take a report or letter drafted by someone else, rewrite bits and submit it as your own work. You will destroy morale, and lose your integrity. If you have some reason for making changes—and this should never be

- ◗ style
- ◗ purest grammar

explain it to the author and, if you eventually disagree, add your own note and sign that addition but leave the original unmolested and signed by your subordinate. Whether you fool the boss or not I don't know, but he'd be pretty dumb if you did.

Cardinal rules of Chapter 6

DO	*DON'T*
● judge on performance alone	● take excuses for poor performance
● promote initiators	● protect poor managers; expose them
● promote heavyweights	● believe anyone who says he is busy
● sack young incompetents	● put a 'demarcation' man into planning
● move older low flyers sideways	● talk too much when interviewing
● use formal assessment to pick winners	● promise anything even by implication
● praise when it's due	● nag
● set specific duties and dates	● be sarcastic
	● intimidate
	● lie
	● plagiarize

7. *Career pointers*

Responsibility

Early in your career get into a job where you have to make decisions and it is just not possible to talk problems over with your boss, who is 300 miles off. After a while in such a post you will find you can get through twice or three times the work of those at head office. Or, of course, you will become an ineffective drone. Do you want everyone to find out which one you are?

Measurability

Take a post that is measurable, and if possible geographically identifiable, so that you can take responsibility.

Enterprise

Take a post where there has been a tradition of mediocrity —where previous incumbents have almost been 'sent to Coventry'—and lift it out of the mud.

Scope

Move horizontally to get experience elsewhere. It is unusual for a man to be promoted over his boss, but he can sometimes tack around him.

Tactics

Read up on interviewing techniques so that you understand just what an interviewer expects of candidates.

Mobility

Don't stay in a job for too long, hoping that by doing it well the job will be uprated. You are expected to do it well. By starting slow and working up pace over a year or two you will fool no one.

Independence

Paddle your own canoe. Don't hang your hat on the boss moving on. He may not move or, worse still, even when close to retirement age he may not be replaced due to organizational change. Don't hitch your canoe to any other.

Decisiveness

It is totally unnecessary to overlap in a new post with the departing incumbent by more than a day or two. You're probably confident enough to feel that you are going to improve things anyway, and if the man is going further up the ladder or retiring, you can phone him if you really must. To be nominated to take over months before the due date is of little use—you won't be able to take decisions until you are in the saddle.

8. So what's it all about

That problem: do something about it NOW—not tomorrow.

Operate from the basis given in this book. You're human, so you'll have to break a rule now and then. But on the whole it is a pretty efficient base from which to start.

Don't think everything here applies to other jobs and not to yours. If you do you've wasted your time and money (if you didn't borrow the book from a library). I can just hear you saying: 'Ah, but he never had a job like mine, with all my problems'. You think not?

On the other hand, don't think that I can do all that I recommend. In fact I am often in astonished admiration of my colleagues in their performance under some of these headings. I fail miserably in many of them, but I am working on it, slowly and with reluctance.

To each of my colleagues: I hope you don't think you are the one person who brought this to mind. All the characters are imaginary . . . we all know that you are the one person with none of these faults.

Don't lose heart. In 0·001 per cent of cases, top managers come from those who do not do one single thing advocated in this book. Someone else may write a book on how to progress in that stream—but it's a complete enigma to me.

UE